Lesson Plans Writing

How to Write a Good Lesson Plan and Avoid Common Mistakes

Neil Karper

Lesson Plans Writing
How to Write a Good Lesson Plan and Avoid
Common Mistakes
by Neil Karper

ISBN 978-0-9866426-1-6

Printed in the United States of America

Copyright © 2010 Psylon Press

Latest books by Psylon Press:

100% Blonde Jokes
R. Cristi
ISBN 978-0-9866004-1-8

Choosing a Dog Breed Guide
Eric Nolah
ISBN 978-0-9866004-5-6

Best Pictures Of Paris
Christian Radulescu
ISBN 978-0-9866004-8-7

Best Gift Ideas For Women
Taylor Timms
ISBN 978-0-9866004-4-9

Contents

Introduction

Welcome to lesson plans wrriting. Whether you are an education student, a new teacher or simply an established teacher looking for guidance on creating more effective lesson plans, you will find a wealth of material presented in this guide. It will highlight the key points related to establishing a lesson plan, including each of the individual steps involved in lesson plan development. In addition, there are templates that you can use for creating your own lesson plans.

Let's get started!

Chapter 1

The Basics of Lesson Planning

Before you can even begin to plan a lesson, there are several critical points that will need to be considered as well as several questions you will need to ask.

First, you must consider what it is that you want to teach. This will need to be based upon your school or state standards and the essential knowledge and skills you need to impart to your students. In addition, you must keep in mind the grade level you are developing the lesson for while also following the time estimate for the allotted time available for that particular lesson.

After you have the topic you can then begin focusing on how you want to teach that topic. If you do not use state standards to assist you in developing your topic, it is a good at least to refer to them to find out the specific standards which your lesson plan can meet. By having your lesson plan in alignment with the state standards, you will be in a better position for proving its necessity and worthiness.

It will also help in ensuring your students are learning what is required by the state. If you are able to correlate the lesson plan to the standards, make sure you record links to those standards in your actual lesson plan. You should make a point to include a title for your lesson plan that will properly reflect the topic you are teaching.

Preplanning

The preplanning phase is crucial in the development of a lesson plan. Keep the following in mind during this phase:

- Make sure you understand the subject matter that you will be teaching.

- List important key concepts, facts, vocabulary terms or skills you plan to cover in the lesson.

- Identify the outcomes or goals you want students to achieve.

- Have a clear idea of what it is that you want students to learn.

- The object must contain content, a behavior and criterion so that you will be able to write in detail what has been learned from the lesson and how well the students grasp it.

- The lesson must include an objective that the students can demonstrate a particular skill.

- Make sure you will be able to determine if the objective of the lesson was met.

- The lesson must include both narrow and broad objectives. The broad objective is the overall goal, while the narrow objective is what the less teaches the students to accomplish.

- The lesson should indicate what is learned in the lesson.

- All objectives in the lesson should be measurable.

As you get started planning the lesson, ask yourself the following questions:

- Where are my students going?

- How are my students going to get there?

- How will I know when they have arrived?

Now it is time to begin thinking about the categories that will form the organization for the lesson plan.

Goals

The goals of a lesson plan determine the aim, rationale and purpose for what you and your students will actually do during class. This section of the lesson plan can be used for expressing intermediate goals that will draw upon prior plans and activities while also setting the stage to prepare students for future activities. Goals are commonly written as broad unit goals that adhere to either state or national curriculum standards.

Ask yourself these questions:

- What are the broad objectives or goals of the curriculum or unit plan?

- What are my goals for this unit?

- What do I expect students to be able to do by the end of this unit?

Objectives

To ensure your lesson plan will teach precisely what it is that you want, you must develop objectives that are clear and specific. Keep in mind that objectives should not be activities that will be actually used in the plan. Instead, they should be learning outcomes based on activities. For example, if your desire is to teach your students how to add 5 + 7, your objective may be that "students will know how to add 5 + 7" or more specifically "the students will demonstrate how to add 5 + 7."

Objectives must also be directly measurable, which means that you will be able to ensure you can tell whether the objectives have been met or not. There can be more than one objective for each lesson plan.

You can also make objectives more meaningful by including both narrow and broad objectives. Broad objectives would more resemble goals and would also include the overall goal for the lesson plan. For instance: to gain familiarity with adding three numbers together. The specific objectives would be more like the first objective we looked at. For example: "the students will demonstrate how to add the numbers 5 + 7 + 3 together."

This section will also focus on what students will actually do in order to acquire further skills and knowledge. Objectives for a daily lesson plan should be drawn from the broader goals of the unit plan.

Ask yourself the following questions:

What will my students be able to do during this lesson?

Under what conditions will the students' performance be achieved?

What is the criterion on which satisfactory achievement of the objectives will be judged?

How will students demonstrate they have learned and now understood the lesson plan objectives?

Writing the Objectives

Now that you have the state standards and your own learning goals, you will be prepared to develop the objectives for that unit. Remember that objectives should be written beginning with "Students will learn to…" or with the verb "Observe……"

Keep in mind that objectives should be measurable and specific because you will need to asses the students over these objectives later. The following list of verbs can be helpful in writing measurable and specific objectives.

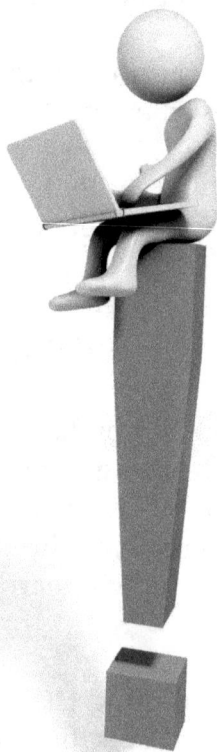

Verb Objective List

Apply	Infer
Appraise	Interpret
Arrange	Judge
Assemble	Justify
Build	Label
Calibrate	List
Categorize	Locate
Change	Measure
Classify	Modify
Combine	Name
Compare	Organize
Compose	Outline
Compute	Perform
Construct	Plan
Contrast	Predict
Create	Produce
Critique	Proofread
Defend	Read
Define	Recall
Demonstrate	Recognize
Describe	Record
Develop	Reflect
Differentiate	Relate
Discuss	Revise
Edit	Rewrite
Evaluate	Select
Experiment	Show
Explain	Solve
Extend	Summarize
Formulate	Verify
Generalize	Write
Identify	

Prerequisites

Prerequisites can be beneficial when you are gauging your students' readiness. They allow you as well as other teachers to replicate your lesson plan as well as to factor in other necessary preparatory activities in order to ensure students will be able to meet the objectives of the lesson plan.

Examples:

- What must students already be able to do prior to this lesson?

- What concepts must be mastered in advance of this lesson to accomplish the objectives?

Materials

Early in the lesson plan you should include the materials that will be needed for that lesson. By doing so you will ensure that should someone else ever need to use your lesson plan they will know ahead of time what materials they will need. Make sure you are specific in regards to everything that will be needed for the lesson.

There are actually two functions to this section. Not only does it assist other teachers in determining the amount of prep time, resources and management will be needed to carry out the lesson plan, but it also ensure the necessary books, materials, resources and equipment will be ready at the appropriate time. It will be most useful to include a complete list of materials, including full citations for any books or texts used, as well as worksheets and any other materials be included.

Example:

• What materials will be needed?

• What books or textbooks will be needed? (include full bibliographic citations)

• What should be prepared in advance? (common in science classes)

Lesson Description

This section of the lesson plan will provide the opportunity for you to share your experience, thoughts and any other advice you may have with other teachers who may use the lesson plan at a later date.

Example:

- How did your students like it?

- What is unique about this lesson plan?

- What level of learning is covered by this lesson plan?

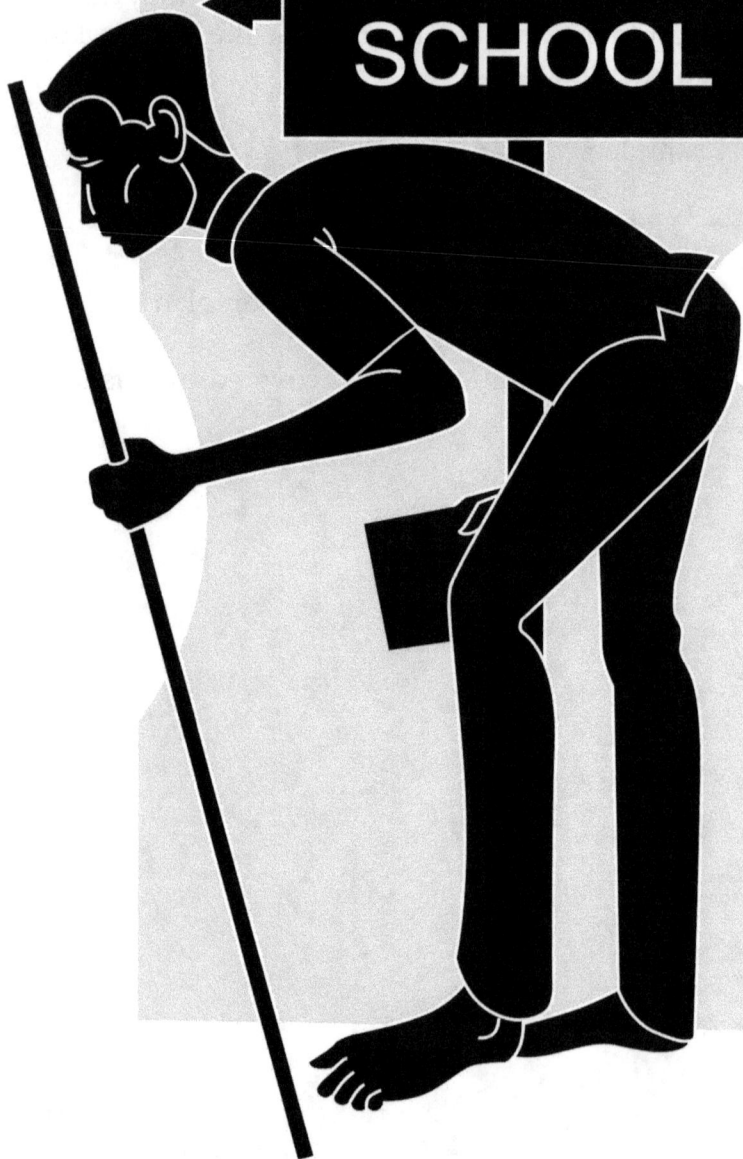

OLD AGE
SCHOOL

Lesson Procedure

The next step in the process is to write the step-by-step procedures that will need to be performed in order to reach the stated objectives. Keep in mind that you do not have to include every single word you will say or everything little thing you will do, but the procedure section should include all of the relevant actions you will perform.

For example, in the 5 + 7 lesson plan, you might have the following procedures:

1. Teacher gives each student 5 unifix cubes

2. Teacher asks the students to write down the number of unifix cubes they have on paper (5)

3. Students write then write a + sign below the number 5 like this:

5
+

4. The teacher will then pass out 7 more unifix cubes to each student.

5. Students will be asked to write down the number of unifix cubes they were just given. They should write this number below the 5 they previously wrote so that it now looks like this:

5
+ 7

6. Students should then draw a line beneath the 7.

7. Students will then count the number of unifix cubes they have total and write this number beneath the 7, like this:

```
   5
 + 7
 ____
  12
```

8. Teacher will ask students how many cubes they had in the beginning, how many they were given to add to that number and how many they had in total after receiving the 7 additional cubes.

This section of the lesson plan offers a step-by-step description regarding how to easily replicate the lesson plan as well as achieve the objectives of the lesson plan. This section is primarily intended for the teacher and will also offer tips and suggestions regarding how to move forward with the implantation of the lesson plan. It will also focus on what the teacher as well as the students should be doing during the lesson plan.

Introduction

Consider the following questions when writing the introduction to your lesson plan:

- How will I introduce the ideas and objectives of this lesson?

- How will I gain students' attention and motivate them to hold their attention?

- How can I tie lesson objectives with student interests and prior classroom activities?

- What will be expected of students?

Main Activity

Consider the following questions when writing the main activity of the lesson plan?

- What is the focus of the lesson?

- How will I describe the flow of the lesson to another teacher who will replicate it?

- What do I need to do to facilitate learning and manage the various activities?

- What are some good and bad examples I can use to illustrate what I am presenting to students?

- How can this material be presented to make certain each student will benefit from the learning experience?

Independent Practice

After you have completed the procedures for the lesson plan, it is a good idea to offer the opportunity for independent practice among the students. For instance, students might be given time to add a variety of numbers of different unifix cubes.

Closure or Conclusion

Ask yourself the following questions when writing the closure or conclusion of your lesson plan:

- What will I use to draw the ideas together for students at the end of the lesson?

- How will I provide feedback to students to correct any misunderstandings and reinforce learning?

Follow up Lessons/Activities

Ask yourself the following questions when writing the follow-up lessons or activities:

- What activities can I use for enrichment and remediation?

- What lessons can be used to follow this lesson?

Assessment/Evaluation

The next part of developing the lesson plan is the assessment or evaluation section. You may see some lesson plans that do not include a section for assessment, but some form of evaluation should certainly take place to determine whether objectives have been achieved.

The important part of developing the assessment is to ensure the evaluation specifically measures whether or not objectives were reached. Therefore, there should exist a direct association between the objectives and the evaluations. Based on the example of adding two numbers together, you might have students add two single digit numbers together on paper by using the cubes as a guide. Remember that the goal of the assessment or evaluation section is to ensure that students have arrived at the intended goal. You will need to gather some evidence in order to evaluate this. This is typically done by gathering the students' work and then by assessing that work, perhaps by utilizing a grading rubric based on the objectives of the lesson plan. Another option would be to replicate some of the activities that were practiced in the lesson. You might also quiz students on the concepts related to the lesson plan.

Keep in mind that you should provide the opportunity for students to practice what they will be assessed on. You should never introduce any new material at this point. In addition, make a point to avoid asking any higher levels questions if students have not yet had an opportunity to practice what is presented during the lesson.

Ask yourself the following questions when developing the assessment or evaluation section of the lesson plan:

- How will you evaluate the objectives that were identified?

- Have students practiced what you are asking them to do for evaluation?

Adaptations

Keep in mind that adaptations should also be made for any students who might have learning disabilities as well as extensions for others. The best way to approach this is by using specific adaptations for specific students by taking into account their individual differences and needs.

It is also a good idea to include a connections section in the lesson plan that will demonstrate how the lesson plan can be integrated along with other subjects. For instance, you might have students color a picture of five blocks and then seven more blocks in order to integrate art in with the lesson plan as well.

Chapter 2

Common Mistakes in Writing
Lesson Plans

Developing effective lesson plans is a continual process of evaluating and looking at where you can make improvements. There are several common mistakes that many teachers make when writing lesson plans. Your lesson plans can be improved by carefully thinking about what the lesson plan is intended to accomplish.

Mistake #1
The lesson plan objective does not specify what it is that the student will do that can actually be observed. Keep in mind that the objective should be a description of what the student will do that will form the basis for assessing the learning that has taken place. A poorly written objective will lead to a faulty assessment.

Mistake #2
The assessment section of the objective is not connected to the behavior that is indicated in the objective. The assessment section of the lesson plan is a description which describes the way in which the teacher will determine whether the objective of the lesson plan has been accomplished and to what degree.

Mistake #3
The materials specified in the lesson are irrelevant to the activities described in the lesson plan. You need to make sure that the list of materials should be kept in line with what it is that is actually planned.

Mistake #4

The instruction the teacher will engage in is not effective for the grade level of the student. In some cases the 'hook' the teacher uses to grab the student's attention is uninspired and ineffective. It is imperative that the hook is interesting for students and is also not too long.

Mistake #5

The student activities described in the lesson plan do not contribute in an effective and direct way to the lesson objective. The activities should always be analyzed to determine whether they will contribute in a meaningful way to what it is that the lesson is intended to accomplish. Activities should not be given simply for the purpose of keeping students busy.

Mistake #6

The pre-assessment of student is inconsistent or not specified with what it is that is necessary in order for the lesson to be successful. The pre-assessment section refers to the statement of what a student will need to know or be able to do in order to accomplish the expectations of the lesson.

Mistake #7

The content of the lesson plan is not detailed enough. It is imperative to ensure that all of the important facts are specific regarding what is being taught.

Mistake #8

In some cases, it is possible to plan too much when developing lesson plans. Do not try to squeeze an entire semester's worth of work into one or two lessons. Recognize that there is a limit regarding how much you can teach within the amount of class time available to you. Make sure you are prepared to split lessons into several different parts if you find there is not enough time to cover everything.

Mistake #9

You can also be too rigid in developing your lesson plans. You must make sure that you have left enough flexibility so that your students may ask questions as necessary and be able to work at their own page. Do not insist that you must follow a precise structure if things do not go as you have planned. Flexibility will allow you to deal with issues as they occur.

Mistake #10

Not planning enough can also be a mistake. If you have free time left over at the end of a class period it could be an indication that you did not plan the lesson as thoroughly or on a comprehensive enough level. To avoid this problem try to plan to have some additional materials you can teach or something the kids can do when you reach the end of the lesson. If you do not need to use it, that is fine; you can use it in a future lesson. If you do need it, you will have it.

Chapter 3

Assessing your Lesson Plan

To determine whether your completed lesson plan is effective, ask yourself the following questions:

- Does my lesson plan permit adjustments or accommodations for students with different abilities and learning styles?

It does without saying that most teachers today have students of varying learning styles and abilities. The instructional method(s) planned for a specified less must take into account the abilities and learning styles of all students. The ability range for students can be quite significant, including emotional handicaps, cognitive disorders, physical handicaps, etc. Teachers must have an awareness of this and take these into account when developing lesson plans.

- Does my lesson plan encourage students to become involved in learning activities on a continual basis?

Instructional procedures and activities should not simply descriptions of what the students and teacher will do. An effective teacher will be able to make adjustments in their instruction based on the feedback they receive from students in order to keep students involved and focused.

- Does my lesson plan allow for adequate coverage of the content to be learned for all students?

The best way to approach this is to consider the least amount of content or material that students should learn in order to indicate they have gained some level of mastery.

- Does the lesson plan allow for monitoring of student progress?

Consider how you will monitor student progress throughout the lesson. There are many ways this can be accomplished and it is up to you to determine the best way to monitor the progress of your particular students in that given lesson. The purpose of such monitoring is not only to collect information regarding student progress but to also utilize the information in order to make changes in the procedures.

- Does the lesson plan allow for adequate assistance of students who have not learned from the first procedure?

Keep in mind that not all students will 'get it' the first time. The reality of the situation is that some students will fall behind and will not grasp the material the first time and you will need to consider how you are going to address that. You must also consider what you will do with the students who did master the material while you working with those who did not. One option would be to provide students who did master the material with additional work or enrichment exercises, allowing you time to work with students who need extra help.

- Does the lesson plan provide sufficient practice to allow for the integration and consolidation of skills?

It has often been said that practice makes perfect and any effective lesson plan should allow time for adequate practice of the skills to be mastered in the lesson. There is simply no substitute for honing skills other than actually practicing them. In some cases it can be difficult to actually practice certain skills and in these situations the best option is to have the students explain what they know.

Chapter 4

Guidance in Writing Activities

One of the most frequent problems that many teachers encounter when writing lesson plans is writing the activities section of the lesson plan. Below are examples of activities to help guide you in this process.

Apply a Rule
In response to the question, "Is clck an English word?" the student would reply, "No, because it has no vowels. All English words must have at least one vowel."

Classify
He could be asked to identify literary forms according to style such as poetry, drama, novel, etc.

Compose
The student could be asked to compose a haiku.

Construct
From the description provided in the textbook, the student might be asked to construct a model of the Jamestown settlement.

Demonstrate
The student might be asked to demonstrate a certain scientific property with a science experiment.

Describe
The student might be asked to describe the culture of a particular Native American tribe.

Diagram
The student could be asked to diagram the parts of the sun.

Distinguish
The student could be provided with a list of nouns and pronouns and asked to distinguish between them.

Estimate
The student might be asked to estimate the number of pencils contained within a box.

Identify
The student might be asked to identify all the vowels in the alphabet.

Interpret
The student might be asked to interpret a passage of literature.

Locate
The student might be asked to locate, in time, the Victorian Period.

Name
The student might be asked to name the parts of speech.

Order
The student might be asked to order a series of events from a specific story.

$$\int_2 f(w)\,dw = 0 \ (|1-z|)$$

$$\int_2^z f(w)\,dw = \sum_{n=0}^{\infty} \frac{a_n}{n+1}\left(z^{n+1} - 2^{n+1}\right)$$

$$z' \to 1$$

$$\int_2 f(w)\,dw = \sum_{n=0}^{\infty} \frac{a_n}{n+1}\left(1 - 2^{n+1}\right)$$

$$\int_2^z f(w)\,dw = \Sigma_1 + \Sigma_2$$

$$N = [1/|1-z|]$$

$$\Sigma_1 = \sum_{n=0}^{N} \frac{a_n}{n+1}\left(1 - 2^{n+1}\right) \qquad \Sigma_2 = \sum_{n=N+1}^{\infty} \frac{a_n}{n+1}\left(1 - 2^{n+1}\right)$$

$$\Sigma_2 = \sum_{N+1}^{\infty} 0\left(\frac{1}{n^2}\right) = 0\left(\frac{1}{N}\right) = 0\left(|1-z|\right)$$

$$-z^{n+1} = (1-z)(1+z+\ldots+z^n) = (1-z)(n+1) - (1-z)^2$$

$$\{n + (n-1)z_n + \ldots \ z^{n-1}\} = (1-z)(n+1) + 0\left(|1-z|^2 n^2\right)$$

$$(1-z)\sum_{n=0}^{\infty} a_n + 0\left(|1-z|^2 \sum_{n=1}^{\infty} n|a_n|\right) = (1-z)S_\infty +$$

$$+ 0\left(|1-z|^2 N\right) = (1-z)S_N + 0\left(|1-z|\right)$$

State a Rules
The student might be asked to state a rule regarding a scientific property.

Translate
The student might be asked to translate a passage from a Shakespeare play into modern day English.

Classify
The student might be asked to classify materials based on their physical properties.

Construct
The student might be asked to construct a model of the solar system.

Describe
The student might be asked to describe the events that occurred within a literary selection.

Diagram
The student might be asked to diagram the life cycle of a caterpillar.

Evaluate
The student might be asked to evaluate which material is the best conductor for electricity.

Identify
The student might be asked to identify which materials would be most attracted to a magnet.

Interpret
The student could be asked to interpret a map.

Measure
The student might be asked to measure a specific amount of liquid in cubic centimeters.

Name
The student might be asked to name the parts of a plant.

Predict
The student might be asked to predict the ecology of an region based on the soils and climate in that area.

Solve
The student might be asked to solve an equation.

Translate
The student might be asked to translate a sentence from English to Spanish.

Glossary

Affective Domain - Refers to the area of learning that deals with students' attitudes, interests, feelings, etc. and focuses on the emotional attitudinal and value goals for students. There are five sub-categories of this domain:

- Receiving
- Responding
- Valuing
- Organization
- Characterization

Anticipatory Set (focus) – Refers to a short activity that focuses the students' attention before the actual starts. Can be used during a transition or when students first enter the classroom. Handouts may be given to students when they first enter the classroom or a review question might be written on the board.

Block Plans - Refers to daily plans that demonstrate the scope and sequence of a learning unit in addition to learning activities, general objectives, resources and evaluation.

Checking for Understanding (CFU) – Refers to a process in which the teacher uses different questioning strategies to determine whether the students comprehend the information and how to pace the lesson, such as whether it is time to move forward or back up.

Closure - A review or wrap-up of the lesson.

Cognitive Domain - Refers to an area of educational objectives that contains objectives related to intellectual tasks such as applying, recalling, analyzing, comprehending, synthesizing and evaluating information.

Guided Practice – Refers to a process in which the teacher leads the students through the necessary steps to perform the required skills.

Independent Practice – Refers to the process in which the teacher allows the students to practice on their own.

Individualized Education Plan - Refers to a learning program that teachers, parents and a qualified school official assist in developing for a student with special needs. The IEP sets forth the goals, services and teaching strategies for that student.

Instructional Planning - Refers to a process in which a teacher determines how to best to select as well as organize a learning experience to maximize achievement.

Input – Refers to the skills, vocabulary and concepts the teacher imparts to the students.

Modeling (show) – Refers to the process of the teacher demonstrating what a finished product will resemble.

Purpose (objective) – Refers to the purpose of the lesson, why the students should learn the material and what they will be able to do when they have mastered the objective.

Unit Plan - Refers to a plan for learning a major topic within a course. Commonly learned over a period of weeks and limited to one topical area

Blank Lesson Plan Format

Your Name
Date
Grade Level:
Subject:

Objectives and Goals:
-
-
-

Anticipatory Set (approximate time):
-
-
-

Direct Instruction (approximate time):
-
-
-

Guided Practice (approximate time):
-
-
-

Closure (approximate time):
-
-
-

Independent Practice:
-
-
-

Required Materials and Equipment:

-
-
-

Assessment and Follow-Up:

-
-
-

Weekly Schedule

Name:
Grade:
Date:

Notes:

Weekly Log

NAME:_____ DATE:_____

Subjet:					
Math					
English					
Science					
History					
Special Projects					

Comments:

Lesson Plans

	Monday	Tuesday	Wednesday	Thursday

Friday	Lists	Memorandum

Sample Lesson Plan 1

Author(s):
Grade Level: 5th
Integrated disciplines: Language Arts, Social Studies, Technology

Standards:

By the end of the 5th grade, students will identify the main idea and supporting details in what they have read.

By the end of the 5th grade, students will be able to identify and apply knowledge of the text as well as organizational elements to analyze nonfiction.

By the end of the 5th grade, students will be able to identify similarities and differences across a different 8th grade reading selections.

By the end of the 5th grade, students will demonstrate the ability to analyze media, films, nonfiction works.

By the end of the 5th grade, students will write using standard English for punctuation, usage, sentence structure, spelling, capitalization, etc.

By the end of the 5th grade, students will be able to write compositions with focus, supporting details and related ideas.

By the end of the 5th grade, students will revise and edit descriptive compositions.

By the end of the 5th grade, students will demonstrate the use of multiple forms to write for different audiences and purposes.

By the end of the 5th grade, students will demonstrate the ability to use self-generated questions, summarization, note taking and outlining while learning.

By the end of the 5th grade, students will participate in group discussions by asking questions and contributing information.

By the end of the 5th grade, students will use multiple presentation styles for specific audiences and purposes.

By the end of the 5th grade, students will identify information gained and complete tasks through listening.

Objectives:
1. Students will read Number the Stars to learn about the problems children experienced during war time as a result of Nazi occupation and the Holocaust on Jewish citizens at that time.

2. Students will demonstrate their understanding of Number the Stars through their interpretation of factual material as well as their personal feelings towards the material.

3. Students will discuss with their classmates specific passages and ideas introduced from in the book to help further their understanding of the text.

4. Students will demonstrate their knowledge and practice of the six traits of writing in their daily journals.

5. Students will be given the opportunity to read silently and aloud in class to improve their skills in reading.

6. Students will improve their vocabularies through the vocabulary words introduced and studied in the book.

7. Students will answer questions on a study guide to demonstrate their comprehension and interpretation of the text.

8. Students will produce a final project that demonstrates their understanding of the text and further explores the historical significance of the period.

9. Students will practice their listening skills in class and discussion groups.

Assessment:

1. The students will write daily in journals on their feelings regarding a variety of pictures displayed using proper spelling, sentences and grammar using the six traits of writing. Students will be graded based on a rubric.

3. The students will read Number the Stars and answer the questions on the study guide as assigned by the teacher with 85% accuracy or better.

4. The students will learn vocabulary words via context clues and/or looking them up in the dictionary and will pass vocabulary quizzes with scores of 85% or better.

5. The students will participate in various small group discussions based on Number the Stars. They will hold various roles in their small groups and actively participate. Assessment will be through teacher observation.

6. The students will choose a final project from a list provided by the teacher and will present their final project to the class. The students will show a greater understanding of the Holocaust and the effects of this historical event on the world and will be graded on a supplied rubric.

Materials:

- Pictures may include:
  - Star of David
  - Train Cars
  - Concentration Camps
  - Nazi Soldiers
  - Adolf Hitler
  - Broken windows of store fronts following Kristallnacht, etc.

- Copies of pre-study survey for each student in the class.

- Copies of reading study guide for each of the students in the class.

- Copies of Number the Stars for each student and the teacher.

- Copies of Vocabulary Words each day for students.

- Copies of Quizzes for Vocabulary Words Dictionaries

- Copies of final project explanations along with rubrics for grading.

Procedures

Learning Activities
What the Teacher will do: The teacher will show pictures at the beginning of each class in order to get the students prepared and thinking about WWII and the Holocaust.

The teacher will direct reading, review reading and sometimes read aloud in class from Number the Stars.

The teacher will review the study guide and readings each day with the students for understanding of the text.

The teacher will set up discussion groups and during the course of the reading.

The teacher will provide students will vocabulary words. Students will define vocabulary words through context clues, or by looking up in the words in a dictionary. The teacher will assess understanding of vocabulary words through occasional quizzes.

The teacher will assign the final projects for the students, which will include the student's choice of one of the following:

- Design a web quest for the class on elements of Number the Stars.

- Create a graphic organizer for Number the Stars.

- Create a Time Line showing how the dates in the novel corresponded with major events in history.

Write a report on the importance of Number the Stars in helping people to understand the Holocaust.

What the Students will do:

The students will write daily journals on their feelings towards various pictures displayed using proper sentences, spelling, grammar and etc.

The students will participate in a pre-study survey for the teacher.

The students will read Number the Stars and answer the questions on the study guide as assigned by the teacher.

The students will learn vocabulary words via context clues and/or looking them up in the dictionary and will pass vocabulary quizzes.

The students will participate in various small group discussions based on Number the Stars.

The students will choose a final project from a list provided by the teacher and will present their final project to the class.

Provision for special needs:

Accommodations will be made in accordance with student IEP requirements as required by the district for any student. In addition the technology projects were added to the final project list in order to accommodate the one dyslexic student in the class who shows a preference for computer based learning.

References: NA

Closure: Students will present their final projects to the class.

Sample Lesson Plan
The Bill of Rights

Unit 3, Chapter 11
Materials: Textbook - The Americans
Procedures:

Bellringer
Have students list their rights as American citizens in their notebook.

Instruction
Have students share and discuss their answers from the bellringer question.

Explain to students that the Bill of Rights was added to the Constitution to protect the rights of states and individuals. The Federalists promised the Anti-Federalists they would add it in order to get their support for ratification of the Constitution. Discuss the key concepts below and have the students give examples of each amendment.

Key Concepts to discuss

• That the first 10 amendments to the constitution make up the Bill of Rights.

• The First amendment protects the freedom of speech, religion, and the press; the right to petition the government and to assemble.

• The Second amendment protects the right to bears arms.

• The Third amendment protects American citizens from having to house soldiers during peacetime in their homes.

• The Fourth Amendment protects Americans from illegal searches and seizures. A search warrant is needed to search a citizen's property.

• The Fifth Amendment gives citizens the right to a grand jury; protects from double jeopardy and self-incrimination right to due process of law and protection in cases of eminent domain.

• The Sixth amendment ensures a person a fair and speedy trial in criminal cases.

• The Seventh amendment states that a person can have a jury trial in civil cases if they are suing for at least $20.00.

• The Eighth Amendment protects from high fines, high bail, and cruel and unusual punishment.

• The Ninth Amendment states that people and states have rights that are not listed in the Constitution.

• The Tenth amendment says that all powers not given to the national government (Delegated powers) are given to the states (Reserved powers)

Activities:
Ask students to take notes during the class discussion of each amendment and draw a picture or a symbol to represent the right or protection given in the amendment. Students will also give an example of each right or protection.

Closure:
Students can respond to the following prompt: The most important right to me is _____ _____ because it _____
_____
_____.

Assessment/Homework:
A) Students can complete a Bill of Rights quiz.
B) Given a list of situations, students will analyze them and apply the appropriate amendment from the Bill of Rights for homework.

Where to Buy this Book

You can buy this book on Amazon. Just go to amazon.com (or your local Amazon site if available) and search for "**Lesson Plans Writing by Neil Karper**".

You can also order it at any bookstore. Just give them the IBSN below:

ISBN 978-0-9866426-1-6

www.ingramcontent.com/pod-product-compliance
Lightning Source LLC
LaVergne TN
LVHW021545080426
835509LV00019B/2843